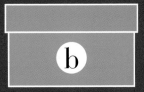

b

bootism: a shoe addict's handbook

by michael duranko and penina goodman
illustrations by penina goodman

EBURY
PRESS

First published in 2003 by Andrews McMeel
Publishing

1 3 5 7 9 10 8 6 4 2

ISBN: 0091897556

Bootism

First published in the UK in 2004 by Ebury Press,
Random House, 20 Vauxhall Bridge Road, London
SW1V 2SA

Random House Australia (Pty) Limited, 20 Alfred
Street, Milsons Point, New South Wales 2061, Australia

Random House New Zealand Limited, 18 Poland
Road, Glenfield, Auckland 10, New Zealand

Random House South Africa (Pty) Limited, Endulini,
5A Jubilee Road, Park Town 2193, South Africa

The Random House Group Limited Reg. No. 954009
www.randomhouse.co.uk
www.bootism.com

A CIP catalogue record for this book is available from
the British Library.

Papers used by Ebury Press are natural recyclable
products made from wood grown in sustainable forests.

Printed and bound in Singapore by Tien Wah.

THIS BOOK IS DEDICATED TO TINA,
A LIFELONG BOOTIST

My friend, lover and inspiration
—Michael

A friend and shopper extraordinaire
—Penina

The Search for Sole

The Bootist quest for chic, style and the perfect black pump comes from lightening your purse and filling every one of your cupboards. Nirvana is attained by channelling the principles of

b

Bootism into a perfect harmony. The Bootist repeats a daily mantra that money is no object and style precedes comfort. Bootists eternally search for a larger cupboard and constantly beg the question, "Who the hell is Mary Jane?"

are you a bootist?

are you a bootist?

yes, no, or maybe?

are you a bootist?

1. do you forget people's names but remember their shoes?

2. do you have more than ten pairs of black shoes?

3. do you often use the words "love" and "shoes" in the same sentence?

4. do you have a system for displaying shoes in your cupboard?

5. on the way to the supermarket, have you ever ended up at the shoe shop?

6. are shoes the most important part of completing an outfit?

7. do you have a standing pedicure appointment?

8. do you know the next season's shoe trends before they hit the shops?

9. have others expressed concern about your interest in shoes?

10. do you daydream about shoes?

truths and vows

you can never have
too many shoes.

style is everything.

4 truths

3

bootism is not a destination,
but a journey through life
in a dynamite pair of shoes.

4

price is not part of the
purchasing decision.

I will shoe shop daily.

I will honour my collection.

I will revere Manolo Blahnik.

3 vows

rules to live by

a Bootist shall not kill . . .
unless someone is about to snatch
the last pair on sale in your size.

a Bootist shall not steal . . .
though begging and borrowing are
acceptable.

**a Bootist shall not misuse sex
appeal . . .** now let's be honest
here, the strappier the sandal and
the higher the heel, the easier to
seduce him.

a Bootist shall not tell lies . . .
but you can misplace the receipt.

**a Bootist shall not speak of
others' errors or faults . . .**
however, judging their shoes
is different.

existence as your shoe self

YIN: the purchase

YANG: The compliment: "Where did you get those?"

Bootists
know they are
not whole until
they have found
the SHOE that
completes the
outfit

bootists are

defined by

their shoes.

meditation = shopping

the adrenaline of bootism is impulsiveness

spontaneous and impulse purchases nourish the bootist

be current.
shop today. shop tomorrow.

bootist reality:
prepare to pay top price.

experience duality:
purchase shoes in multiple colours.

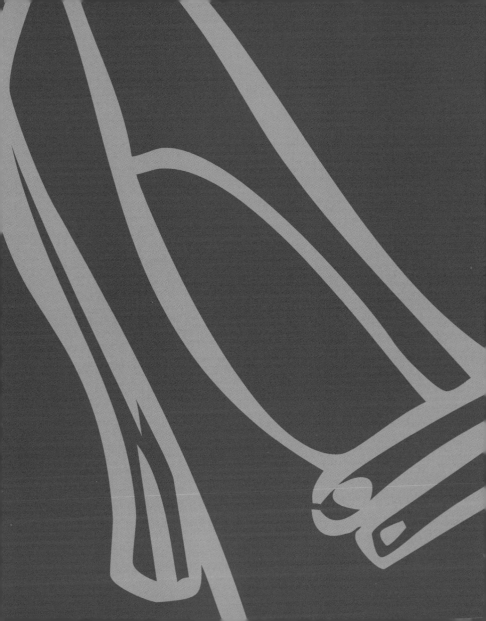

your temple, your shoe shelves

your temple

YOUR CLOSET

THE
BIGGER
THE
BETTER

REPEAT DAILY:

There is always room for one more pair.

There is always room for one more pair.

There is always room for one more pair.

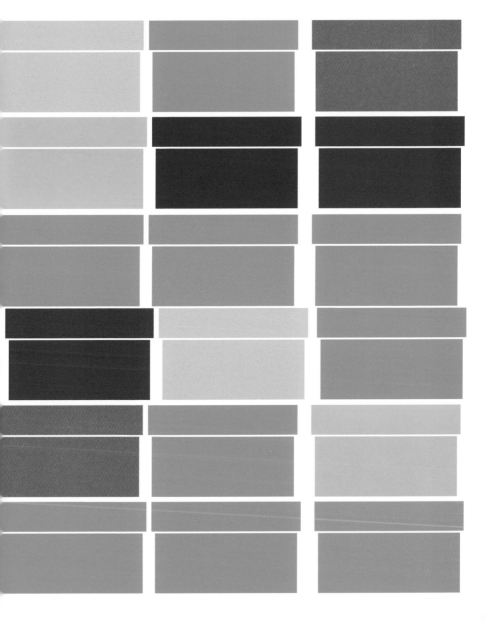

existing with the nonbeliever

nonbelievers think
the bootist will grow
out of the obsession, but
the bootist is obsessed with
growing the collection.

the bootist must:

Masterfully hide receipts.

Strategically enter the home after a successful shopping excursion.

Feign the return, a performance worthy of an Academy Award.

Be able to answer, "Do you really need another pair of black shoes?"

celebrity bootists

THE SHOE

MUST GO ON!

"My name is Sarah Jessica and I own well over one hundred pairs of Manolo Blahniks. I'm not proud of my habit, but it's what I do with my disposable income."
—*Sarah Jessica Parker*

"It's got to be comfortable and come *off* fast."
—*Kim Cattrall*

"The qualities I find sexy in a person include intelligence, humour, and really good shoes."
—*Sting*

"Shoes are not an accessory; they're an attribute."
—*Christian Louboutin*

"I am a simple man."
—*Jimmy Choo*

"I try to never get into the trap of trends."
—*Manolo Blahnik*

"I did not have three thousand pairs of shoes,
I had one thousand and sixty."
—*Imelda Marcos*

PUT ON YOUR
RED SHOES
AND DANCE THE BLUES.
—David Bowie

sole mates

HEART AND SOLE

THE B♥♥TIST KNOWS
WHEN LOOKING FOR
MR RIGHT, HE MAY
HAVE TWO LEFT FEET.

WHO IS THE BOOTIST'S PERFECT PAIR

The Bootist is looking for the one who sweeps her off her feet, leaves her spinning head over heels, and never stops playing footsie. . . . Why, the Harvey Nichols' shoe salesman is a perfect match, and she's already on his speed dial.

Not a good fit?

ONE TWO
BUCKLE YOUR SHOE.
THREE FOUR
KICK HIM OUT THE DOOR!

the corporate bootist

CLIMBING THE CORPORATE LADDER

Get your foot in the door.

Put your best L. K. Bennetts forward.

Be two steps ahead:
Shop the autumn season in Milan.

Make sure the client is footing the bill.

Knock their socks off:
Kick up new heels at the board meeting.

**You think on your feet, but
even better in a new pair of heels.**

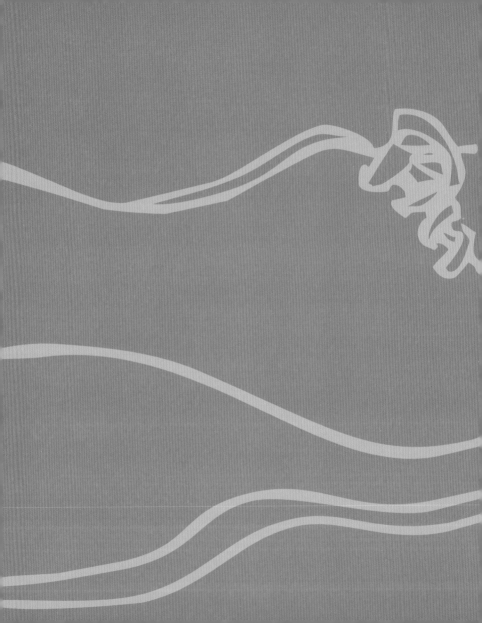

grandma's shoes

grandma's shoes

When I was very little
All the grandmas that I knew
All walked around this world
In ugly grandma shoes.

You know the ones I speak of,
Those black clunky heeled kind,
They just looked awful
That it weighed upon my mind,

For I knew, when I grew old,
I'd have to wear those shoes,
I'd think of that, from time to time
It seemed like such bad news.

I never was a rebel,
I wore saddle shoes to school,
And next came ballerinas
then the sandals, pretty cool.

And then came spikes with pointed toes,
Then platforms, very tall,
As each new fashion came along,
I wore them, one and all.

But always, in the distance,
Looming in my future, there,
Was that awful pair of ugly shoes,
The kind that grandmas wear.

I eventually got married,
And then I became a mum
Our kids grew up and left,
And when their children came along,

I knew I was a grandma
And the time was drawing near
When those clunky, black, old lace-up shoes,
Were what I'd have to wear.

How would I do my gardening
Or take my morning hike?
I couldn't even think about
How I would ride my bike!

But fashions kept evolving
And one day I realized
That the shape of things to come
Was changing right before my eyes.

And now, when I go shopping
What I see fills me with glee
For, in my jeans and Reeboks
I'm comfy as can be.

And I look at all these teenage girls
And there, upon their feet
Are clunky, black old grandma shoes,
And they really think they're neat.

—*Anonymous*

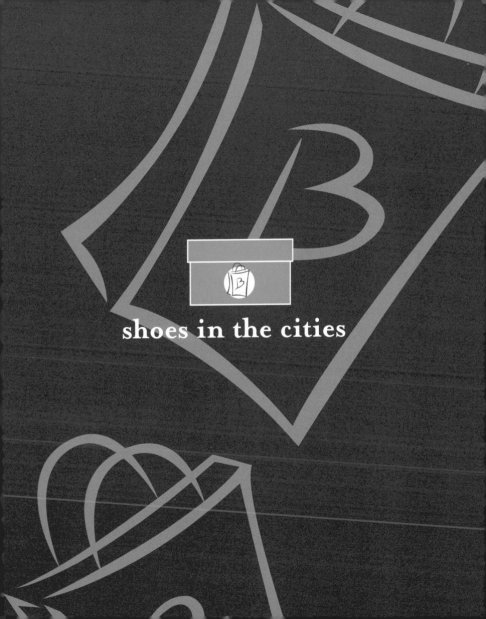

shoes in the cities

the bootist lives locally but
SHOPS GLOBALLY!

LONDON

Shelly's

Johnny Moke

Emma Hope

LOS ANGELES

Fred Segal

Top Shoes

Diavolina II

NEW YORK

Geraldine

Otto Tootsie Plohound

Jeffrey

PARIS

Christian Louboutin

Rodolphe Menudier

Free Lance

SYDNEY

Shoo Biz

Gary Castles

Evelyn Miles

MILAN

Cesare Paciotti

Vicini

Zeta Calzature

bootisms

BOOTISM IS NOT ABOUT NEEDS, It's ABOUT WANTS + DESIRES.

mantramantra

you can

never be

too rich,

mantramantra**mantra**mantra

believe   too thin,

in the

power of   or have too

the sole.   many shoes.

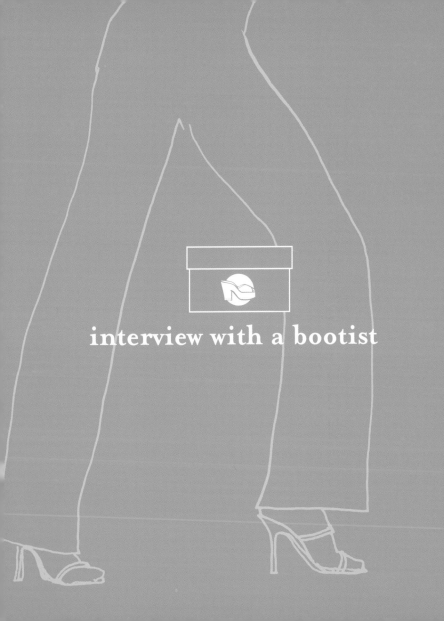

interview with a bootist

interview — lisa k. |favourite shoe season: autumn ——————

" your favourite shoe store? Emma Hope, Sloane Square. **standing pedicure?** Yes. Fabulous, my best investment or indulgence, and very therapeutic. Really, I've bonded with everyone at the salon: they're like family, and my pedicurist gives me advice on everything from work to clothes to buying our house. **shoe storage?** Two ways, well, three. Plain ones on the floor that I wear a lot, like mules. Basic slip-ons—you know, the ones that wouldn't look good on a rack. Then I have stack racks for display shoes and two hanging racks for my smart ones. And that doesn't include my flip-flops, trainers, and boots in the coat cupboard. **adrenaline rush for autumn or spring collection?** Autumn. No doubt. **"**

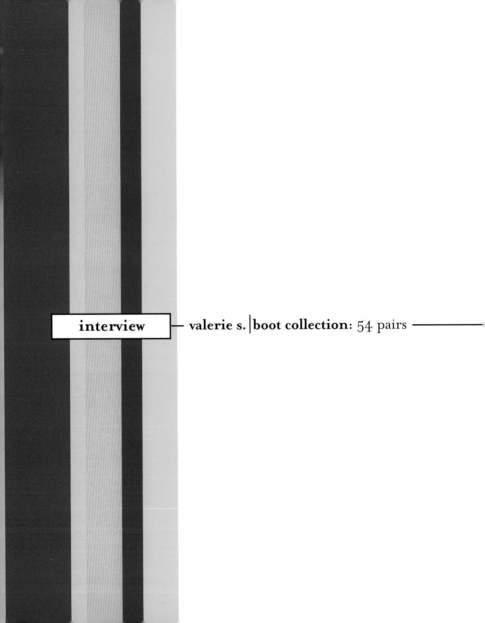

interview — **valerie s.** | **boot collection:** 54 pairs ——————

" are new shoes a religious experience for you? If I find a great pair it is! Or if I am travelling and find a great new shop or boutique, it's certainly uplifting. do you have a relationship with your shoes? Yes! They are displayed so when I get dressed, I have every option available to me. It's important, and it's empowering. do you consider your shoes an investment? I can always justify a shoe purchase. For me, shoes are a long-term investment. **"**

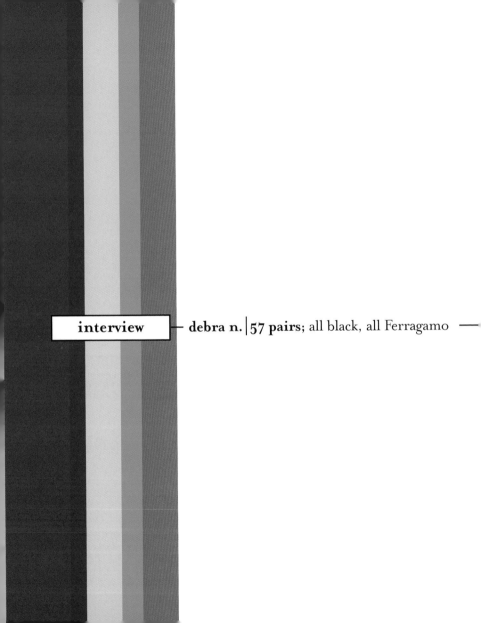

interview — **debra n.** | **57 pairs**; all black, all Ferragamo —

" when you meet someone for the first time, and forget their name, do you remember their shoes? Only the good, the bad, or the ugly. I can always tell if I want to see a guy again with one look at his shoes, either too nerdy, too slick, too sloppy, too sporty, or just right. do you dream of shoes? YES! Well, shoes or shoe shopping? I dream more of shoe shopping. I dream of trying on shoes because that soothes me. I shopped today, I bought shoes. I needed one pair and I tried on three, well, four. have you ever bought a pair of shoes and then bought a second pair the same day? Oh, yeah! Ohhh, yeahhh! At the same time or later. I've done both. "

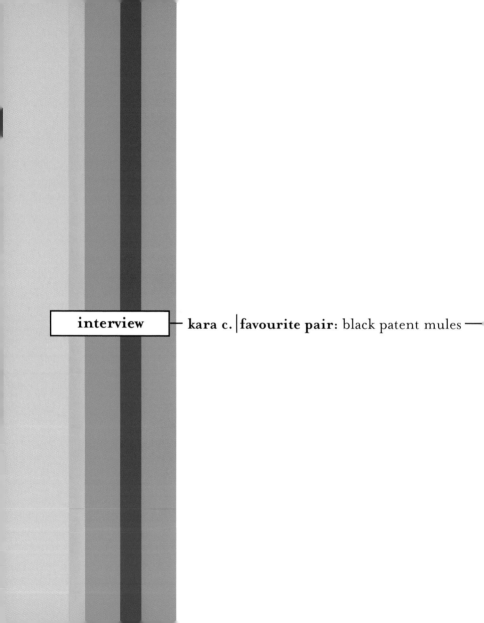

interview — **kara c.** | **favourite pair**: black patent mules —

" can you think of a bad time to shop for shoes? I can always slip my feet into a pair of shoes. Shoe shopping is so much easier than shopping for clothes. Plus, my favourite place to meet people is the Selfridges shoe department. Does that count? do you dream of shoes? I fall asleep by thinking of outfits and what goes together. Shoes are a very important part of my dreams. I must visualize my shoes, and sometimes if I can't, I won't be able to fall asleep. Other times, in my dreams I will find myself wearing the wrong shoes and I'll wake up. do you take better care of your shoes or your car? I wish I took better care of my shoes. I consider it a love/hate relationship, and you always take for granted the one you love. **"**

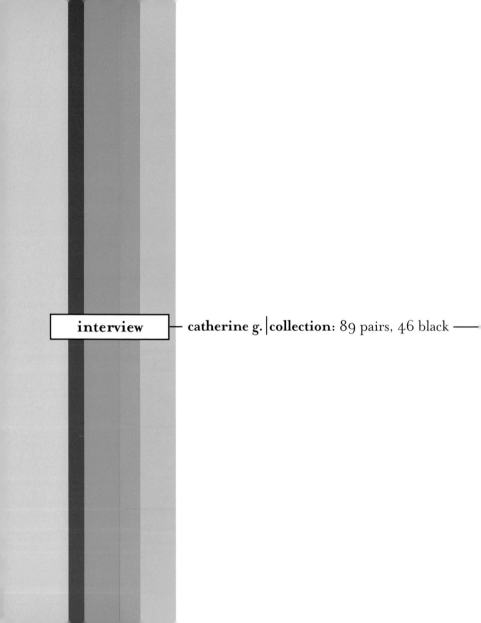

interview — **catherine g.** | **collection**: 89 pairs, 46 black —

" your favourite shoe store? **Liberty.** do you take better care of your shoes or your car? **My shoes (giggle) probably my shoes, yeah, my shoes. I take good care of my car but better care of my shoes.** when you meet someone for the first time and forget their name, do you remember their shoes? **Usually, yeah, I do, I confess. I remember if they were wearing memorable shoes. If I don't remember their shoes, they weren't fun shoes or just basic.** "

interview ⊢ **lisa s.** │ **collection**: always growing...

" favourite shoe store? My gosh, I don't have a favourite, but I like Fenwick and Harvey Nichols. But I can pretty much find something I like anywhere, but I do really LOVE Fenwick. do you consider your shoes an investment? Yes. However, the return is not monetary but sexiness and confidence. An investment in well-being, not financial. shoe storage? I keep them in boxes, only because I don't have room for a display rack. do you have a relationship with your shoes? It's completely to the heart. I wake up and I think about what to wear and what I wear revolves around my shoes. have you ever bought a pair of shoes and then bought a second pair the same day? Of course! Duh! "

bootist astrology

THE STARS TELL YOU WHAT YOUR SHOE
DECISIONS SAY ABOUT YOU, YOUR LOVE LIFE,
AND YOUR FAVOURITE SHOE SALESPERSON.

aquariuspiscesariestaurusgeminicancerleovirgolibrascorpiosagittariuscapricorn
aquariuspiscesariestaurusgeminicancerleovirgolibrascorpiosagittariuscapricor
naquariuspisce°°°°°°°taurusgeminicancerleovirgolibrascorpiosagittariuscaprico
rnaquariuspi ... .usgeminicancerleovirgolibrascorpiosagittariuscapric
ornaquarius .scesarie aure geminicancerleovirgolibrascorpiosagittariuscapri
cornaquari spiscesaries rus minicancerleovirgolibrascorpiosagittariuscap
ricornaqu iuspiscesaries rusg minicancerleovirgolibrascorpiosagittariusca
pricornaq ariuspiscesariest usge inicancerleovirgolibrascorpiosagittariusc
apricorna nariuspiscesariesta isgen nicancerleovirgolibrascorpiosagittarius
capricorna nariuspiscesariesta sgem icancerleovirgolibrascorpiosagittariu
scapricorna ariuspiscesariestau sgemin cancerleovirgolibrascorpiosagittari
uscapricorn u iuspiscesariestau sgemin ancerleovirgolibrascorpiosagitta
riuscapricorn qua spiscesariestau sgemin ancerleovirgolibrascorpiosagitt
ariuscapricorn quariu scesariestaur gemini ncerleovirgolibrascorpiosagit
tariuscapricorn quar sp esariestaurus aminic cerleovirgolibrascorpiosagi
ttariuscapricorn qr sp sariestaurusg minica erleovirgolibrascorpiosa
gittariuscapricor na ua iuspi sariestaurusgem erleovirgolibrascorpios
agittariuscapricorn qu riuspi sariestaurusgemini leovirgolibrascorpio
sagittariuscapric r ac iariuspi sariestaurusgeminicance virgolibrascorpi
osagittariuscapr to n quariuspi sariestaurusgeminicancerleo irgolibrascor
piosagittariuscap.. naquariusp. sariestaurusgeminicancerleo irgolibrasco
rpiosagittariuscapricornaquariusp ariestaurusgeminicancerle irgolibrasc
orpiosagittariuscapricornaquariuspis iestaurusgeminicancerl virgolibras
corpiosagittariuscapricornaquariuspisces estaurusgeminicancerl eovirgolibra
scorpiosagittariuscapricornaquariuspiscesariestaurusgeminicancerleovirgolibr
ascorpiosagittariuscapricornaquariuspiscesariestaurusgeminicancerleovirgolib
rascorpiosagittariuscapricornaquariuspiscesariestaurusgeminicancerleovirgoli
brascorpiosagittariuscapricornaquariuspiscesariestaurusgeminicancerleovirgo

ARIES

March 20–
April 19

Rams need to lead the way, which means all the world will be checking out your footwear. And because you charge full-steam-ahead into life, stiletto heels are simply not an option. Many Arians admit to a lifelong obsession with men's oxfords and vaguely militaristic styles while secretly coveting the skimpiest of pumps.

TAURUS

April 20–
May 20

Earthy Bulls need to feel grounded, and what better way to accomplish that than with butter-smooth leather shoes? You need quality, you need contemporary styles that don't scream "fashion victim" and you need *more* now. When it comes to footwear you fancy, money's no object. Quick, to the shops!

GEMINI

May 21–
June 20

It's no secret you need endless stimulation and variety in all areas of your life, and your shoe collection is no exception. Your feet must reflect your constantly changing moods and opinions, which is why you'd rather have fifty pairs of forty-pound shoes than ten pairs of expensive ones.

CANCER

June 21—
July 22

Selecting shoes, like everything else in your life, is less about the hipness of a shoe than what kind of emotional response it elicits. Only Cancer girls could say that red makes you feel sexy, black makes you understand the very meaning of elegance and straps can catapult you back in time to 1981.

LEO

July 23—
August 22

The Queen of the Jungle needs the finest footwear to shield her protective paws. And spending a bundle on a single pair of boots or sandals really does make you feel lionhearted. Bored silly with plain black court shoes, you're the answer to that question frequently asked by shoe amateurs: "Who could get away with something this wild?"

VIRGO

August 23—
September 22

If there's one thing that gets your goat, it's the automatic association of the phrase "sensible shoes" with your sign. Hel-lo! You've got some kick-ass cowboy boots and a pair of Kim Novak-esque stilettos right next to the Campers. It's your incredible sense of discrimination that people don't appreciate.

LIBRA

September 23–
October 23

Right after romance and getting together with your twenty best girlfriends is buying new shoes. You can shop till the salesperson drops! And lest others denigrate the talent, you're quick to point out that it's no small feat, so to speak, getting shoes to match every tote, bag and clutch in your other cupboard.

SCORPIO

October 24–
November 22

Like carefully planted symbols in a nineteenth-century class-struggle novel, shoes say a lot about people—even if you're the only one who can pick up on all the nuances. That's why you'll try on half a dozen pairs with every outfit before you step out of the house. Pointy black boots have a very special place in your heart.

SAGITTARIUS

November 23–
December 21

In your private universe, you worship Jerry Seinfeld and his hundred pairs of brand-new trainers of every style and stripe. But your two "x" chromosomes could never actually permit such behavior. Still, your sporty Converse put comfort over radical style, and "easily removed" is criterion number one.

CAPRICORN

December 22–
January 19

It's only half true that your symbol, the climbing mountain goat, influences your footwear choices. The other half of the equation is your innate sense of style and high fashion, even if you have Chanel taste on a New Look budget. You're happy with a few excellent pairs, in styles that will last longer than a teenager's attention span.

AQUARIUS

January 20–
February 18

Here's where you live up to your eccentric reputation. From those bowling shoes at school to the shaggy-dog look of today, you've always dressed to a different drummer. There's literally no such thing as "too weird," whether that means vertigo-inducing outrageous fashion or flea-market chic.

PISCES

February 19–
March 19

Shoes are your obsession, the Rosetta stone of your secret fantasy life. You can pass by a rack of wildly coloured dresses or a counter laden with exotic beads, but you can't walk by a shoe shop. If a traffic warden were about to write you a parking ticket at the exact same moment you noticed the most perfect pair of strappy sandals, you'd just calculate the cost of the ticket into the price of the shoes.

—by Suzanne Gerber

ABOUT THE AUTHORS

Michael Duranko

Shoe size: US 11
Favourite shoes of all time: Black on white golf shoes, metal spikes, 1990
Extravagant shoe purchase: Red, black, and white high-top Air Jordans, 1984

Duranko lives in Manhattan with his Bootist wife, Tina. He does not think of himself as a religious leader; he is a simple man with a simple message. He has an affinity for Tod's.

Penina Goodman

Shoe size: US 10
Favourite part of her closet: Shelves designed specifically to house and organize her shoe collection
Shoe collection: 90 percent black

Goodman lives in Chicago and admits to being a fashionista with Bootist tendencies. Many of her closest friends live the Bootist life and she is thrilled to collaborate on providing them with a voice. Her shoe attachment is to Saucony Grid Stabils.